cooking

with

MACKIE'S®

A selection of sweet & savoury recipes

Harriet Shaw & Nikki Nangle

Conversion Guide

You may find that cooking times vary depending on the oven you are using.
All the recipe timings and cooking temperatures are based on a fan-assisted oven.
If you are using a conventional oven (non-fan assisted), increase the oven temperature by 15°c.

Producers: Harriet Shaw & Nikki Nangle

Design: John Barrie

Print: Claro Print

Photographer: Ross Byrne

Recipes & food
for photography:
                    Anne Lyburn,
                    Karin Hayhow,
                    Nikki Nangle,
                    Harriet Shaw
                    & Mackie's employees

Props stylist: Paige Quirie & Ross Byrne

First published in 2018 by Mackie's at Taypack Ltd

ISBN 978-1-5272-2528-2

contents

Muscular Dystrophy UK

Fighting muscle-wasting conditions

FOREWORD – Robert Meadowcroft, Chief Executive, Muscular Dystrophy UK

"Muscle-wasting conditions can be devastating, and that's why so many people passionately support the research and services which Muscular Dystrophy UK funds.

We are delighted to count the fantastic team at Mackie's among those supporters, and this book is just the latest delicious example of their hard work to raise funds for us.

By buying this book, you are joining them in supporting the 70,000 people in the UK who have a muscle-wasting condition. Whether you attempt one of their new popcorn creations or rustle up a batch of haggis bon bons, you have already helped fund more world-class research and desperately-needed support for families all over the country.

But you don't have to stop there. You can use these fantastic recipes to take part in our annual Bake A Difference, where the nation's bakers get to work every October to raise funds."

You can find out more on Bake A Difference, and the many other ways you can join the fight against muscle-wasting conditions, at **www.musculardystrophyuk.org**

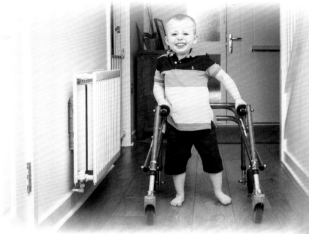

About Muscular Dystrophy UK

Every day counts when you're living with a progressive and potentially life-threatening muscle-wasting condition.

With over 70,000 people in the UK living with muscular dystrophy, Muscular Dystrophy UK is urgently searching for treatments and cures to improve lives today and transform those of future generations. Together, we're pressing for faster access to potential drugs that could transform lives and we're driving change to see better care and support to help people stay active, independent and connected.

We understand that muscular dystrophy changes everything. That's why we're here for anyone who is affected, right from the moment of diagnosis and beyond. We're here to help people take back some control of their lives and to live well with the condition. We understand the everyday challenges of muscular dystrophy, so we're here with information and advice, together with emotional and practical support and a network of local groups and an online community.

With your support we can be here for everyone affected today, tomorrow and beyond.

Together we will bring forward the day when we beat muscular dystrophy.

MACKIE'S
of Scotland

ICE CREAM
Chocolate

OUR fourth-generation family business has been farming at Westertown in rural Aberdeenshire since 1912. We began making ice cream in 1986 when changing trends towards skimmed and semi-skimmed milk left us with a surplus of cream. Mackie's ice cream is now Scotland's no.1 luxury ice cream, one of the top 5 take home tubs across the UK and can be found as far afield as Korea & Taiwan.

While we remain a traditional business making dairy products on the same family farm, we do have some surprising and ground-breaking elements to the way we do that.

Our company vision is "to become a Scottish global brand from the greenest company in Britain, created by people having fun."

Mac Mackie believes that the farm can be a self sufficient renewable energy innovator, and that dream is coming to fruition in a big way – resulting in a range of renewab es from four large turbines, a biomass plant and what was until fairly recently Scotland's largest solar farm, providing over 70% of our energy.

Other technology investments mean that in addition to energy we make our own packaging and the cows milk themselves on robotic milking machinery.

We have diversified into the four product ranges celebrated in this recipe book and most recently launched our first bespoke ice cream parlour,

Mackie's 19.2 – named to reflect the distance from the farm to the parlour in Marischal Square, Aberdeen. There we have a tempting range of over 20 flavours on offer with crepes, waffles, cones and tubs, showcasing the best of what we create on the farm – and where we can trial new flavours or the next "big hairy" new product idea!

We hope that you will have fun with these recipes & that you'll enjoy our products in some delicious new ways.

Please do submit any new recipes ideas to us at **www.mackies.co.uk**

We will reward those we can use with some ice cream, chocolate, crisps and popcorn!

We are here

MACKIE'S
of Scotland

Our product range

Ice Cream

Ice cream is now the cornerstone of our business – the focus for the team on our 1600 acre arable farm, which includes a 450 cow dairy herd. Those ladies supply fresh cream and whole milk helping us to produce more than 11 million litres of real dairy ice cream in a year.

Our most popular flavour remains our first – Traditional – a fresh, smooth & creamy ice creamy with a natural taste. There's no added flavour – not even vanilla – just real ice cream 'made the way it should be'.

The Mackie's ice cream range includes classic and modern favourites, from Honeycomb to Salted Caramel.

We hope that you'll enjoy our Ice Cream as a happy treat or snack, whether served simply on its own, drowned in coffee or topped with sauce, in creative sundaes, as the perfect complement to other delicious desserts or the star in a big birthday party cake.

Chocolate

Delicious chocolate made in Scotland! We refine, conche and temper the beloved treat to create a deliciously smooth and balanced bar.

You can expect the best in natural ingredients, with flavours reflecting those of our top ice creams.

Only the finest quality will work – its so good we've even plumbed an ever-flowing tap of tempered chocolate into our Aberdeen parlour! You will find that Mackie's chocolate melts beautifully so that you can make your own chocolate sauces or try the delicious cakes, brownies or even flavour a savoury stew in this first collection of our recipes.

Mackie's Crisps was founded in 2009 as a joint venture between third generation Perthshire potato farmers, the Taylor family, and Mackie's of Scotland, an Aberdeenshire-based family business renowned for their luxury ice cream.

Combining the Mackies' experience in everyday indulgence with the Taylors' expertise in growing quality potatoes, the company created a premium range of potato crisps, which are now available in around 25 countries worldwide.

Mackie's Crisps are made in Perthshire, Scotland using the best varieties of crisping potatoes.

The company take great pride in their unique gentle cooking method which ensures a great crunch, fresh potato taste and dry texture.

The standard Mackie's Crisps range consists of nine flavours; these include traditional flavours, such as Sea Salt and Mature Cheddar & Onion, as well as Scottish Speciality varieties, such as Flamegrilled Aberdeen Angus and Haggis & Cracked Black Pepper flavour. More recently Mackie's Crisps have launched a range of Ridge Cut crisps, comprising nine additional flavour varieties.

The newest addition to the Mackie's product selection is a range of popcorn. The flavours in this range were developed to complement the existing Mackie's crisps and ice cream products, with an indulgent toffee coated flavour on offer alongside traditional popcorn flavours of Sweet, Lightly Sea Salted and Sweet & Salted.

We are here

Our product range

Popcorn

Mackie's popcorn is made using the finest popping corn to give us our little pops of perfection! Our standard range is lightly sprinkled with seasonings and our more indulgent popcorn has a crispy toffee shell.

Our popcorn can be used as a tasty, crunchy topping for a sundae or cheesecake or an extra addition to rocky road bars, amongst other things!

Straight cut crisps

Our straight cut crisps are cooked gently in high oleic sunflower oil to achieve their unique dry texture. They are made will all-natural ingredients and have no artificial colours or flavourings. Our ever-popular Sea Salt flavour is made with just 3 simple ingredients – potatoes, oil & sea salt.

Mackie's crisps are great straight from the pack as a snack or tipped into a bowl to enjoy with friends – but our recipes will also tempt you to enjoy them as a topping on your macaroni cheese or as a crispy coating for haggis bon bons.

Ridge cut crisps

Our ridge cut crisps are cooked in the same way as our traditional range, but are sliced slightly thicker and hold their seasonings even better for a fantastically strong flavour.

Their deep ridges make them perfect for dipping so we've included a selection of tasty dips in this recipe book.

cooking

with

MACKIE'S®
of Scotland

A selection of sweet & savoury recipes

ICE CREAM

Strawberry Prosecco Float
Easy Baked Alaska
Ice Cream Cake
Affogato
Frozen Clover Club
Whisky Toffee Sauce and Toasted Marshmallows
Honeycomb Ice Cream Sundae

Potato Crisps

Dark Chocolate Tart
Mac & Cheese
Haggis & Bon Bons
Nachos
Haggis, Neeps & Tatties Gratin
Fish Goujons

Dips

Red Onion & Coriander Cream Cheese Dip
Guacamole
Easy Peasy Hummus
Garlic & Herb Dip

Popcorn

Rocky Road
Salted Caramel & Toffee Popcorn Cheesecake
Fruit & Nut Bars
Toffee Popcorn Sundae
Popcorn Marshmallow Bars
Spicy Popcorn Chicken
Popcorn Bark

Chocolate

Flourless Chocolate Cake
Quick Chocolate Mousse
Self-Saucing Chocolate Pudding
Chocolate Chilli Beef Stew
Deluxe Hot Chocolate
Boozy Chocolate Sauce
Chocolate Marshmallow Brown Sugar Fudge

A super simple yet special ice cream cocktail - find an excuse to celebrate!

Strawberry Prosecco Float

Serves: 1

Ingredients:

35ml gin

15ml strawberry puree

5ml fresh lemon juice

Prosecco or Champagne

1 scoop of Mackie's Strawberry Ice Cream

Method:

Shake together the gin, strawberry puree and lemon juice. Pour into glass.

Fill the glass with Prosecco or Champagne and stir gently.

Place a scoop of Mackie's Strawberry Ice Cream on top and serve immediately.

Recipes with ice cream

Easy Baked Alaska

A delicious, easy, yet quite impressive dessert that will certainly impress your guests!

Serves: 6
Prep time: 30 minutes
Cooking time: 10 minutes

Ingredients:

6 tbsp of orange juice

Raspberry jam

Sponge flan case

3 egg whites

200g caster sugar

Pinch of cream of tartar

1 Litre of Mackie's Ice Cream (any flavour)

Method:

Buy a large flan case and a tub of Mackie's Ice Cream!

Soak 6 tbsps of orange juice into the sponge and spread the base with some raspberry jam. Scoop out a litre tub of Mackie's Ice Cream onto the base, keeping it as tightly packed as you can and return it to the freezer for at least half an hour (cover in cling film if you want to leave it overnight).

Pre heat the oven to 230˚C.

In a large bowl, whisk the whites until stiff, then beat in the cream of tartar. Fold in the caster sugar, a tbsp at a time, then whisk at high speed into a thick and shiny meringue.

Take the ice cream flan out of the freezer (remove cling film!) and paste the meringue mix over it – completely seal in the ice cream with meringue mix and decorate it by swirling the meringue with a palette knife. Put back in the freezer for at least an hour or until you are ready to cook.

Bake your creation for about 3-4 minutes. The meringue should set and go golden, but the ice cream will be insulated and still cold. If you have a kitchen blow torch you could add a final touch of colour & avoid leaving the Baked Alaska in the oven for any longer.

Ice Cream Cake

A celebration cake made of ice cream which all ages will enjoy! Ice Cream cakes are fun & guaranteed to go down a treat at birthday parties. It's easy to make and you can make it your own - with any ice cream flavour, your favourite sweeties & different decorations. Best consumed within a few days.

Tip:
For an adult version mix a creamy liqueur into the softened Traditional ice cream for the "icing" and refreeze the day before.

Prep time: 15 minutes and 3 hours freezing

Ingredients:

3 - 4 tubs of Mackie's Ice Cream

A mixture of sweets - Maltesers, Crunchie, marshmallows, chocolate of any shape or size.

Method:

Gather your ingredients – you will need three or four flavours (different colours to look good) of Mackie's Ice Cream and a variety of sweets – e.g Maltesers, Crunchie pieces, Smarties, chocolate buttons, marshmallows. Line a medium or large plastic bowl with cling film – allow the cling film to hang over the edge of the bowl as you will need it to wrap it all up later. You also need a big spoon (this works better than an ice cream scoop).

Thaw the tubs of ice cream for about 10 minutes – or just until it begins to soften. Spoon the first flavour of ice cream into the bowl, squash it down and cover with a layer of sweets.

Add further layers of ice cream and sweets. The last layer should be ice cream and will be the base of your cake. You might like to add biscuit for an extra base or use Mackie's Chocolate Ice Cream which is the firmest.

Smooth and flatten the ice cream as this will be the base of your cake - and cover with cling film. Put it in the freezer for at least 3 hours.

Take out a tub of Mackie's Traditional Ice Cream and allow it to soften. Then tip the Ice Cream cake out onto a plate and remove the cling film.

Cover the cake with the soft Traditional Ice Cream – it looks like icing.

Decorate the cake as you wish. Slice to serve immediately or pop it back in the freezer until you are ready to eat.

This classic Italian dessert, ice cream drowned in coffee, is a perfect way to finish off a meal.

**Tip:
Add a
dash of your
favourite spirit
or liqueur on
top.**

Affogato

Serves: 4
Prep time: 10 minutes

Ingredients:

200ml made-up, hot, strong espresso coffee

Mackie's Madagascan Vanilla Ice Cream

Method:

Make the espresso coffee, which will be enough for 4 little after-dinner coffee cups.

Put a generous scoop of ice cream into each cup – and drown (the literal meaning of Affogato) each with coffee and serve while warm and melting.

A frozen take on this pretty-in-pink classic cocktail - a perfect treat to start a summer party or relax in the garden!

Frozen Clover Club

Serves: 2

Ingredients:

100ml Gin

60ml raspberry puree

40ml fresh lemon juice

2 scoops of crushed ice

2 scoops of Mackie's Raspberry Ripple Ice Cream

Garnish:

Fresh raspberries

Method:

Pour and place all ingredients (apart from the chocolate) in blender, blend until there are no lumps and the cocktail has a smooth, thick texture.

Pour into glasses and garnish with fresh raspberries. Serve immediately.

Whisky Toffee Sauce and Toasted Marshmallows

A delicious way to jazz up a bowl of ice cream!

Tip: Use a traditional sundae glass for a surprise snack or treat.

Serves: 4
Prep time: 15 minutes

Ingredients

75g butter

100g soft brown sugar

125ml double cream

50ml whisky

50g marshmallows

Mackie's Traditional Ice Cream

Method:

Put butter, sugar and cream in a thick based saucepan and heat gently until the sugar has dissolved. Add the whisky and leave to cool slightly.

Put marshmallows on a baking tray and grill under a hot grill or use blow torch until they are golden and sizzling.

Scoop ice cream into individual dishes, drizzle over the whisky toffee sauce and top with toasted marshmallows.

Honeycomb Ice Cream Sundae

A special sundae with some of our favourite ingredients, honeycomb ice cream, a delicious homemade butterscotch sauce and chopped buttered pecans.

Serves: 4
Prep Time: 30 minutes

Ingredients:

Butterscotch Sauce

100g unsalted butter

100g light brown sugar

100g golden syrup

1/2 tsp lemon juice

150ml double cream

Vanilla pod

Buttered Pecans

25g unsalted butter

150g pecan nuts

1/4 tsp flaky sea salt

To Serve

Mackie's Honeycomb Ice Cream

Mackie's Traditional Ice Cream

Ice cream wafers

Method:

Preheat the oven to 180°C.

Start making the buttered pecans. Melt the butter in a large frying pan, then remove from the heat and add the pecans. Stir until they are well-coated in the melted butter and sprinkle with the salt.

Tip onto a baking tray lined with greaseproof paper and spread them out evenly.

Place in the oven and toast for 10-12 minutes, stirring once during baking. Remove from the oven and set aside to cool completely. When cooled roughly chop the nuts.

While the nuts are cooling make the butterscotch sauce by placing the butter, brown sugar, golden syrup and vanilla pod (scraping the seeds from the pod and adding them to the mixture) in a small saucepan over a medium heat.

When the mixture is simmering gently, remove from the heat and add the lemon juice to taste, stir in the double cream, remove the vanilla pod and set aside to cool slightly.

When you are ready to serve - pour a little butterscotch sauce in the bottom of each sundae glass and add a few of the chopped pecans followed by a scoop of ice cream.

Repeat in layers until you reach the top of the glasses. Top with a final drizzle of sauce and chopped pecans and a wafer. Serve immediately.

Dark Chocolate Tart

This is certainly a pudding with a twist! We've added sea salt crisps to the base of this tart, which compliments the darkness of the rich Mackie's 70% Dark Chocolate.

Serves: 6

Prep time: 30 minutes

Cooking time: 10 minutes / 2 hours cooling

Ingredients:

Tart:

1 x 150g pack of Mackie's Sea Salt Crisps (crushed until fine)

90g butter (melted)

30g of flour

1 tbsp golden syrup

For the topping:

300ml double cream

2 tsps caster sugar

50g unsalted butter

200g Mackie's 70% Dark Chocolate (broken into squares)

Pinch of sea salt flakes and Mackie's Traditional Ice Cream to serve

Method:

Preheat oven to 180°C. Crush crisps in food blender until fine, add in the melted butter, spoon of syrup and flour and pulse together until combined.

Press the potato chip crust into the bottom and sides of a 9-inch tart pan. Transfer to the pre-heated oven and bake for 10 minutes. Remove from the oven and set aside to cool.

Put the cream & sugar into a pan and bring to the boil.

Take off the heat when this begins to boil.

Now, stir in the butter and chocolate squares until both are fully melted.

Pour this chocolate-y mixture into the tart case and leave for minimum 2 hours to set. Sprinkle with sea salt flakes before serving with a scoop of Mackie's Traditional Ice Cream!

It doesn't get much more comforting than homemade macaroni cheese. This also works well with our Mature Cheddar & Onion crisps for added cheese!

Mac & Cheese

Serves: 6
Prep time: 30 minutes
Cooking time: 20 minutes

Ingredients:

225g dried Macaroni

50g butter

45g plain flour

275g grated mature cheddar cheese
(save a few handfuls for the top!)

50g parmesan cheese

750ml milk

1 x 150g packet of Mackie's Crispy
Bacon Crisps (crushed)

Method:

Cook the Macaroni as per packet instructions (but taking 2 minutes off cooking time) and drain.

Melt the butter in a saucepan, add the flour and stir in well to a smooth paste, gradually add the milk and cook until the mixture boils and thickens, add the cheeses and salt and pepper.

Mix the Macaroni with the sauce and pour into an ovenproof dish.

Bake for 10 minutes at 180°C then remove and add grated cheese followed by crushed crisps. Bake for another 10 minutes until browned and bubbling!

These make the perfect Scottish style canape! Use vegetarian haggis for a veggie option and enjoy with a creamy sauce.

Haggis Bon Bons

Makes: 12 bon bons
Prep time: 15 minutes
Cooking time: 20 minutes

Ingredients:

1 small Haggis

1 beaten egg

1 x 150g pack of Mackie's Haggis & Cracked Black Pepper Crisps (crushed)

Method:

Remove the Haggis from the skin and break into pieces, then form into bitesize balls.

Roll the ball in the beaten egg and then coat with the crushed crisps.

Place all the bon bons on a baking tray and bake at 180°C for 20 minutes.

Serve with a creamy peppercorn sauce .

For a taste of Mexico with a Scottish twist try our nachos with Mackie's Ridge Cut crisps! Our spicy Sweet Chilli Crisps work well with the creamy cheese and cool soured cream.

Nachos

Tip:
For a more substantial meal you can even add our beef chilli (page 68) on top too!

Serves: 4
Prep time: 5 minutes
Cooking time: 5 minutes

Ingredients:

150g pack of Mackie's Ridge Cut Crisps (we recommend Sweet Chilli flavour!)

300ml tub of soured cream

Tub of salsa

Tub of guacamole (see our recipe on page 42 to make this homemade)

200g cheddar cheese (grated)

Chilli pepper & coriander leaves to garnish

Method:

Lay out your Mackie's crisps on a baking tray. Top with grated cheese and pop in the oven at 200°C for around 4-5 minutes until it's all melted.

Top with dollops of the soured cream & salsa and slices of chilli if you can handle some heat! Serve with guacamole and a sprinkle of coriander leaves.

Haggis, Neeps & Tatties Gratin

Looking for a Burns Night supper? This recipe brings together all the Burns essentials in a comforting dish, topped with Mackie's Crisps for a special crunch. We recommend serving with peppercorn sauce or gravy!

Serves: 4
Prep time: 45 minutes
Cooking time: 20 minutes

Ingredients:

450g haggis

300g turnip (cut into small chunks)

500g potato (maris piper or similar)

2 tbsps double cream

40g butter

1 x 150g pack of Mackie's Haggis & Cracked Black Pepper Crisps

Method:

Cook the haggis according to pack instructions.

Peel and chop the potatoes and turnips into large chunks then boil in separate pans for around 30 minutes until soft. Drain well.

Add butter and pepper to the turnip then mash until smooth.

Add cream to the potatoes and mash until smooth.

When the haggis is cooked, slit it open and put in the bottom of a gratin dish.

Top with turnip and potato adding a little more cream to the mash if required.

Crush crisps in the packet and sprinkle on top of the gratin.

Place in the oven at 180°C and cook for around 10 minutes.

Take out and top with crisps before baking for another 10 minutes until piping hot.

Fish, potatoes, salt & vinegar – can you get a more classic combination? These fish goujons have a lovely crisp-y coating and are best enjoyed with ketchup or tartare sauce!

Fish Goujons

Makes: 12 strips
Prep time: 20 minutes
Cooking time: 15 minutes cooling
15 minutes cooking

Ingredients:

450g of firm white fish (filleted, skinned and cut into strips)

½ of a 150g pack of Mackie's Sea Salt & Vinegar Crisps (crushed)

50g breadcrumbs

50g plain flour

1 large egg, beaten

Method:

Mix together the crushed Mackie's Crisps and breadcrumbs and place in a large shallow dish.

Put the beaten egg into another wide bowl and the flour into a third.

One by one, dip the strips of fish into the flour, then into the egg, and lastly cover with the crisp/breadcrumb mixture, pressing it on to make sure it sticks.

Continue until all the fish is coated, then chill it in the fridge for 30 minutes minimum.

Bake the fish goujons in the oven on a preheated tray lined with baking paper at 200°C for 15 minutes until golden.

Serve warm with a squeeze of lemon.

Coriander may not be for everyone but combining it with the tangy red onion and the coolness of the cream cheese gives you the ultimate dip combination! Use extra sweet chilli dipping sauce if you're a fan of spice!

Red Onion & Coriander Cream Cheese Dip

Prep time: 10 minutes
Cooking time: 2 hours chilling

Ingredients:

250g cream cheese

1/2 x small red onion (finely chopped)

2 x tbsps chopped coriander

5 x tbsps sweet chilli sauce

Method:

Place the cream cheese, chopped onion and coriander into a bowl and mix until combined.

Scoop into a bowl lined with clingfilm, smooth over the top and then leave to chill for 2 hours minimum.

Take this mixture out of bowl taking care to keep the shape and turn this upside down onto a large serving bowl.

Pour a generous helping of sweet chilli sauce around the island of cream cheese and serve!

Although this guacamole makes a lovely addition to our nacho dish, it's also very delicious on it's own!

Guacamole

**Tip:
Keep the avocado stone in the guacamole until you're ready to serve, as it stops it from going brown.**

Prep time: 10 minutes

Ingredients:

1 x Avocado

Generous squeeze of Lemon/Lime

½ a small red onion

5 x cherry tomatoes

Handful of coriander

Salt to taste

Method:

Scoop out your avocado and mash it in a bowl, squeezing over your lemon/lime juice to stop it browning.

Finely chop your red onion into small pieces and do the same with the tomatoes before mixing all this together.

Add in a handful of torn up coriander and salt to taste.

Dips

Hummus has got to be one of the most popular dips out there, and our recipe couldn't be easier to make. We drizzled ours with extra virgin olive oil, but you can also top the dip with a sprinkling of paprika for a hint of spice.

Easy Peasy Hummus

**Tip:
This will keep for up to a week in an airtight container in the fridge**

Prep time: 10 minutes

Ingredients:

400g can of chickpeas (drained)

Juice of a large lemon

4 tbsp tahini paste

1 clove garlic (crushed)

3 tbsps Olive oil

½ tsp salt

3-4 tbsps water

Method:

Add the tahini paste, garlic, lemon juice and olive oil into a food processor and mix for about 1 minute. Then add half of the chickpeas and whizz until smooth. Add the remaining chick peas and whizz again until there are no lumps. Slowly add the water until the hummus reaches the right consistency.

Transfer the hummus into a serving bowl and drizzle with olive oil to serve.

Another quick and easy dip to whip up, we recommend serving this with our Sea Salt & Cider Vinegar Ridge Cut Crisps!

Garlic & Herb Dip

Prep time: 10 minutes

Ingredients:

1 x 150g Le Roule garlic & herb cheese (or similar)

2 spring onions, finely chopped

1 tbsp lemon juice

1 small tub (150ml) soured cream

1 tbsp chopped fresh chives to garnish

Method:

Mix all the ingredients together to create the dip, adding a little milk if too thick.

Sprinkle with the chives and serve with a bowl of Mackie's Ridge Cut Crisps.

Dips

This rocky road recipe is gooey, delicious and packed full of different treats.

Rocky Road

Tip:
You can add chopped up glacé cherries and nuts if they take your fancy.

Makes: 12 squares
Prep time: 30 minutes
Cooking time: 1 hour chilling

Ingredients:

50g butter

1 (397g) tin of condensed milk

1 x tbsp of cocoa powder

1/2 bag of Mackie's Sweet Popcorn

200g crushed digestive biscuits

1 tbsp desiccated coconut

100g raisins

50g mini marshmallows

250g Mackie's Chocolate, melted
(dark or milk, whichever you prefer)

Method:

Put the tin of condensed milk into a saucepan over a gentle heat and stir in the cocoa powder and butter until completely melted.

Take off the heat and mix in the popcorn, biscuits, raisins and marshmallows.

Line an 8x6" baking tin with greaseproof paper and put the mixture into it, making sure to level it out.

Top with melted Mackie's chocolate.

Put in the fridge to set for at least an hour.

Turn out onto a chopping board, peel off the paper and cut into squares.

Salted Caramel & Toffee Popcorn Cheesecake

Look no further for a showstopping pudding that tastes divine but takes almost no time! This is nice and easy to whip up and you can add in different flavours and top it with your favourite sauces to make it your own.

Ingredients:

For the base:

130g digestive biscuits

80g melted butter

For the cheesecake:

300ml double cream

60g icing sugar

300g full fat cream cheese

Squeeze of lemon juice

Tsp of vanilla extract

½ jar of caramel sauce

½ bag of Mackie's Toffee Popcorn

8" cake tin with a removable base

Serves: 6

Prep time: 40 minutes

Cooking time: 4 hours chilling

Method:

Whizz up the biscuits until they form a crumb consistency. Mix this all with the melted butter and then press into the bottom of the cake tin. Put in the fridge to cool.

Beat together the cream cheese, lemon juice, vanilla extract and sifted icing sugar until smooth.

Whip the double cream until it forms very light peaks and then fold into the cream cheese mixture.

Smooth this mixture over the biscuit base, before returning to the fridge for at least 4 hours to set.

When you're ready to serve remove the cheesecake and place on a serving plate, before topping with the toffee popcorn and slightly melted caramel sauce.

These fruit and nut bars can be drizzled with Mackie's 70% Dark chocolate to make them slightly more special or simply packed in a box for a filling hillwalking or picnic snack.

Fruit & Nut Bars

Makes: 14 bars
Prep time: 20 minutes
Cooking time: 1 hour chilling

Ingredients:

½ x 100g pack of Mackie's Sweet & Salted Popcorn

100g rolled oats

100g raisins

100g dried apricots, chopped

100g pecan nuts, chopped

150g Dark soft brown sugar

50g toasted sunflower seeds

4 tbsps honey

Method:

Line a shallow tin or dish with clingfilm.
Put the sugar and honey in a large pan and dissolve over a low heat.

Put the dry ingredients into a large mixing bowl and stir until all mixed. Then pour over the sugar & honey mixture and stir until both are fully combined.

Quickly transfer this to the lined tin and press down, this is easiest with dampened hands.

Leave to cool and firm up for about an hour.

Tip out onto a board, remove the clingfilm and cut into bars.

Simply layer hot butterscotch sauce with crunchy Mackie's toffee popcorn and traditional ice cream for this sensational sundae!

Toffee Popcorn Sundae

Serves: 2

Prep time: 20 minutes

Cooking time: 1 hour chilling

Ingredients:

4 handfuls of Mackie's Toffee popcorn (half a 200g pack)

2 squares of good quality chocolate brownies (or even better, homemade!)

4 large scoops of Mackie's traditional ice cream

1/2 jar of butterscotch sauce

Wafer curls to serve

Method:

You will need 2 sundae glasses or large wine glasses.

Spoon in a couple of tbsps of butterscotch sauce to the bottom of your serving glasses.

Put in a handful of toffee popcorn and a scoop of Mackie's traditional ice cream. Repeat this process again before topping your sundae with extra butterscotch sauce.

Pop a brownie on top and then add a wafer curl for decoration. Easy and very delicious!

If you're looking for a simple recipe for a sweet treat then this is the one for you! Use a mixture of pink & white marshmallows to give these bars a baby pink colouring and feel free to decorate with sprinkles to jazz them up!

Popcorn Marshmallow Bars

Makes: 10 bars
Prep time: 20 minutes
Cooking time: 1 hour chilling

Ingredients:

1 x 100g pack of Mackie's Sweet Popcorn

2 tbsp unsalted butter

200g bag of marshmallows

Method:

Melt the butter & marshmallows together over a low heat in a large saucepan.

Take off the heat and mix in the popcorn until fully coated.

Press into a baking tray lined with greaseproof paper.

Put in the fridge for an hour to set before cutting into bars and dust with a topping of icing sugar when done!

These popcorn coated chicken strips make a delicious and light savoury snack. For a spice-free version of this popcorn chicken, simply remove the chilli powder from the recipe.

Spicy Popcorn Chicken

Makes: 8 strips

Prep time: 30 minutes

Cooking time: 30 minutes chilling
20 minutes cooking

Ingredients:

2 skinless chicken breasts, cut into long thin strips

¾ of a 70g pack of Mackie's Lightly Sea Salted Popcorn

Tsp of chilli powder

50g breadcrumbs

50g plain flour

1 large egg, beaten

Method:

Put the Mackie's popcorn, breadcrumbs and chilli powder into a food processor and blend until fine.

Place the popcorn mix into a large shallow dish. Put the beaten egg into another wide bowl and the seasoned flour in a 3rd bowl.

Dip the strips of chicken into the seasoned flour, then into the egg, and lastly cover with the popcorn/ breadcrumb mixture, press it on to help it to stick evenly on the chicken. Continue until all the chicken is coated, then chill it in the fridge for 30 minutes (or you can do this in the morning ready to cook in the evening).

Mix the dip ingredients together and place in a small bowl.

Bake the chicken on a tray in the oven at 200˚C for 15-20 minutes until golden.

Serve warm with the dip and some lime wedges if you wish.

Our popcorn bark is very simple to make and can be customised by topping it with your favourite snacks, fruits & nuts!

**Tip:
This bark can easily be made for a gift by wrapping in cellophane bags and tying with a bow.**

Popcorn Bark

Prep time: 10 minutes

Cooking time: 1 hour setting

Ingredients:

400g of Mackie's Milk Chocolate

50g of Mackie's 70% Dark Chocolate

½ of a 100g pack of Mackie's Sweet & Salted Popcorn

Handful of salted pretzels

Handful of dried fruits

Handful of pecans (or other nuts)

Method:

Place the milk chocolate in a bowl over a saucepan of gently simmering water and slowly melt until completely smooth.

Spread this out on a sheet of baking paper laid on a baking tray with a palette knife, until ~1cm thick.

Whilst the chocolate is still soft add your toppings (which can be whatever you like!)

We've gone for our sweet & salted popcorn, some pretzels, dried fruit & nuts but the possibilities are endless.

Next once the chocolate tray has had a chance to set, melt the small amount of dark chocolate in the microwave on a low heat. Drizzle this dark chocolate over the chocolate bark as a finishing flourish.

Flourless Chocolate Cake

This delicious flourless chocolate cake looks and tastes great - crusty on top with a fudgy centre. Perfect on its own or served with a generous scoop of ice cream!

Serves: 10
Prep time: 30 minutes
Cooking time: 1 hour plus cooling

Ingredients:

200g unsalted butter, plus extra for greasing

200g Mackie's 70% Dark Chocolate

1 tbsp strong coffee

6 large free-range eggs

250g golden caster sugar

70g cocoa powder, plus extra for dusting

Pinch of sea salt

Method:

Preheat the oven to 160°C. Grease a 20cm spring form cake tin with a little butter and line with greaseproof paper.

Rest a medium heatproof bowl over a pan of simmering water on a medium-low heat. Break in the chocolate, roughly chop and add the butter, allow to melt stirring occasionally until smooth and glossy.

Carefully remove the bowl from the heat, stir in the coffee and set aside to cool slightly.

Separate the egg yolks and whites between two large bowls. Whisk the egg whites until soft peaks form.

Add the sugar to the yolks and beat for 7 minutes, or until pale. Sift in the cocoa powder and a pinch of sea salt then gently fold through to combine.

Stir in the melted chocolate mixture; then gently fold through the egg whites until smooth.

Transfer to the tin and place in the hot oven for 1 hour, or until an inserted skewer comes out clean.

Allow to cool completely on a wire cooling rack, serve with a dusting of cocoa powder and fresh berries.

A super easy and quick chocolate mousse using only four simple ingredients - to deliver a real Chocolate hit. (eggs & gelatine free)

Quick Chocolate Mousse

Serves: 4
Prep time: 20 minutes

Ingredients:

150g Mackie's 70% Dark Chocolate

250ml crème fraiche

300ml double cream

25g icing sugar

For Garnish

Whipped cream

Fresh raspberries

Grated chocolate

Method:

Put the double cream and icing sugar into a bowl and whisk with an electric whisk until soft peaks form.

Break the chocolate into small pieces and melt in the microwave (stirring at 20 second intervals).

Once the chocolate has melted, quickly combine with the crème fraiche and stir until fully mixed.

Fold the chocolate mixture into the cream and combine.

Spoon the mousse into individual dishes, garnish with whipped cream, fresh raspberries and grated chocolate.

Recipes with chocolate

A light chocolate sponge with a warm rich chocolate sauce - guaranteed to please any chocolate lover!

Self-Saucing Chocolate Pudding

Serves: 6
Prep time: 30 minutes
Cooking time: 25-30 minutes

Ingredients:

For the pudding

100g melted butter, plus extra for greasing

3 eggs

175ml milk

250g self-raising flour

50g cocoa powder

1 tsp baking powder

150g soft light brown sugar

120g Mackie's 70% Dark Chocolate, finely chopped

120g Mackie's Milk chocolate, finely chopped

For the sauce

300ml water

200g light brown soft sugar

40g cocoa powder

Method:

Preheat the oven to 180°C and butter a two-litre ovenproof dish.

Whisk the melted butter, eggs and milk together in a jug until smooth. Sift the flour, cocoa powder and baking powder into a bowl then stir in the sugar.

Pour the butter mixture into the flour mixture and mix well to a smooth batter. Stir in the dark and milk chocolate and spoon into the prepared baking dish.

To make the sauce, bring 300ml water and the sugar to the boil in a saucepan, then add the cocoa powder and whisk until smooth. Pour over the top of the batter then bake for 25-30 minutes. The top of the sponge will be just firm to the touch.

Serve hot with a scoop or two of real dairy ice cream!

Chocolate Chilli Beef Stew

A rich, warming chilli beef stew with Mackie's 70% Dark Chocolate - the chocolate adds a surprising depth of flavour to the stew.

Prep time: 30 minutes
Cooking time: 3 hours

Ingredients:

2 tbsp vegetable oil

1 kg braising steak, cut into chunks

2 large onions, sliced

4 garlic clove, crushed

2 tbsp tomato purée

1 tsp ground cumin

1 tsp ground coriander

1 tsp cayenne powder

Small knob of butter

2 tbsp plain flour

2 tbsp caster sugar

400g tin chopped plum tomatoes

1 bottle or carton (500g) passata

1 tsp dried oregano

450ml hot beef stock

50g Mackie's 70% Dark Chocolate, broken into pieces

Method:

Heat the oven to 130°C.

Put the oil in a hob-proof casserole set over a medium heat and brown the meat all over. Set aside.

In the same pan, add a little more oil and a knob of butter, then gently fry the onions for 10 minutes until softened. Stir in the garlic and tomato purée, and cook for 1 minute. (add a little boiling water if necessary to stop everything sticking to the pan base).

Add the cumin, coriander, cayenne powder and flour, and cook for 1 minute, followed by the sugar, tomatoes, passata and oregano.

Make up stock with boiling water. Gradually blend in the beef stock and bring to the boil. Return the beef to the pan, stirring into the sauce, season with salt and freshly ground black pepper. Cover and transfer to the oven for 2½ hours, or until the meat is tender.

Stir in the chocolate, and heat gently while stirring into the mix, the sauce should look shiny and rich!

Drain & rinse the red kidney beans in a sieve, then stir them into the chilli pot. Bring to the boil again. Return to the oven for 30 minutes.

Taste again before serving – you may need to add further seasoning.

TIP:
You can also add a tin of kidney beans. This recipe works well on its own as a stew, but also works really well as a pie filling.

Keep warm with this indulgent hot chocolate - comfort in a cup.

Deluxe Hot Chocolate

Serves: 4
Prep time: 2 minutes
Cooking time: 5-10 minutes

Ingredients:

600ml milk

150ml double cream

100g Mackie's 70% Dark or Milk Chocolate, Chopped

For garnish

Mini marshmallows

Grated chocolate

Mackie's Ice Cream

**Tip:
Top with a scoop of ice cream for an extra creamy hit & a nice mix of hot & cold.**

Method:

Pour the milk, double cream and chopped chocolate into a pan. Bring gently to the boil, whisking until smooth. Serve in individual cups or mugs topped with mini marshmallows and a little grated chocolate or with a generous scoop of ice cream.

A simple chocolate sauce for adults - perfect for pouring over ice cream, drizzled over fruit kebabs or served warm over chocolate pudding

Boozy Chocolate Sauce

Any liqueur can be used - Amaretto, Baileys, Cointreau, Drambuie, Gin, Grand Marnier, Limoncello, Vodka, Whisky.

Serves: 3
Prep time: 5 minutes
Cooking time: 10 minutes

Ingredients:

50g Mackie's 70% Dark Chocolate

25g butter

150ml double cream

1 tbsp caster sugar

1 tbsp of liqueur

Method:

Melt the chocolate in a bowl over a pan of barely simmering water until completely smooth.

Heat all of the remaining ingredients (butter, double cream, sugar and liqueur) in a small saucepan until evenly combined. Remove from the heat and stir through the melted chocolate. Serve warm over chocolate pudding, ice cream or both!

Chocolate Marshmallow Brown Sugar Fudge

Who doesn't love home-made fudge - this recipe is simple to make - for yourself or a gift.

Makes: 25 squares
Prep time:
Less than 30 minutes
Cooking time:
Less than 10 minutes

Ingredients:

Vegetable oil, for greasing

70g butter

300g soft light brown sugar

125g evaporated milk

225g marshmallows

300g Mackie's Milk Chocolate, chopped

75g Mackie's 70% Dark Chocolate, chopped

Method:

Grease a 20cm/8in square cake tin with vegetable oil, then line with greaseproof paper.

Put the butter, sugar and evaporated milk in a pan over a low heat and melt gently. Once the sugar has dissolved, add the marshmallows and turn up the heat. Boil the fudge for 5-6 minutes.

Take the pan off the heat and add the chopped chocolate. Leave for one minute; then stir the mixture together until everything is melted.

Pour the mixture into the prepared tin and leave to set for a couple of hours. Once set, remove from the tin and cut into squares.

MACKIE'S *memories*

Four generations of Maitland Mackie, the youngest Mac Mackie is our current Managing Director.

Sir Maitland CBE began milk deliveries from around the Huntly & Aberdeen area in the late 30's.

Mackie's of Scotland is now owned by siblings Kirstin, Mac & Karin Mackie who each have Senior Management positions in the business.

Due to cream surplus arising from a market shift to semi-skimmed milk, Mackie's enter the world of making dairy ice cream in 1986.

Mackie's milkmen established tradition of supplying quality produce to consumers with a range of products "fresh from the farm".

The Taylors at Moncur farm, Inchture back in 1927.

Errol Brickworks, the current site of the Mackie's Crisp factory, dates back to 1870.

Mackie's relocated their crisp factory to Errol in 2013 where they are still based now.

In 2009 the Taylor & Mackie families joined forces and launched Mackie's Potato Crisps!

2018 - Mackie's at Taypack Managing Director, George Taylor, and his son James.

Recipe Index